D1442485

20ᵀᴴ CENTURY ART
1920-40
REALISM and SURREALISM

Please visit our web site at: www.garethstevens.com
For a free color catalog describing Gareth Stevens' list of high-quality books
and multimedia programs, call 1-800-542-2595 (USA) or 1-800-461-9120 (Canada).
Gareth Stevens Publishing's Fax: (414) 332-3567.

Library of Congress Cataloging-in-Publication Data available upon request from publisher.
Fax (414) 336-0157 for the attention of the Publishing Records Department.

ISBN 0-8368-2850-X

This North American edition first published in 2001 by
Gareth Stevens Publishing
A World Almanac Education Group Company
330 West Olive Street, Suite 100
Milwaukee, WI 53212 USA

Original edition © 2000 by David West Children's Books. First published in Great Britain in 2000 by
Heinemann Library, Halley Court, Jordan Hill, Oxford OX2 8EJ, a division of Reed Educational and
Professional Publishing Limited. This U.S. edition © 2001 by Gareth Stevens, Inc. Additional end
matter © 2001 by Gareth Stevens, Inc.

Picture Research: Brooks Krikler Research
Picture Editor: Carlotta Cooper
Gareth Stevens Editor: Valerie J. Weber

Photo Credits:
Abbreviations: (t) top, (m) middle, (b) bottom, (l) left, (r) right

AKG London: pages 3, 4, 6(both), 7(b), 8(both), 9(b), 13(t), 18, 19(tr, b), 20(t), 22(r), 25(b),
  28(both), 29.
Bridgeman Art Library: page 10(t).
Bridgeman Art Library © ADAGP, Paris, and DACS, London, 2000: page 22(l).
Bridgeman Art Library © ARS, New York, and DACS, London, 2000: page 17(t).
Bridgeman Art Library © DACS 2000: pages 7(t), 9(t).
Bridgeman Art Library © Salvador Dali – Foundation Gala – Salvador Dali/DACS 2000: page 24(t).
Bridgeman Art Library © Succession Picasso/DACS 2000: page 26(b).
Corbis: pages 5(t), 10(b), 12(t), 13(b), 14(both), 15(b), 16(both), 20(b), 23(b), 24(b), 26(t), 27(both).
Corbis © ADAGP, Paris, and DACS, London, 2000: page 23(t).
Corbis © Francis G. Mayer: page 15(t).
Corbis © Philadelphia Museum of Art: page 17(b).
Corbis © Salvador Dali – Foundation Gala – Salvador Dali/DACS 2000: page 25(t).
© Palace of Cortes, Cuernavaca, Mexico, USA/Ian Marsell/Mexicolore/Bridgeman: page 19(tl).
Tate Publishing © ADAGP, Paris, and DACS, London, 2000: page 21.
Tate Publishing © Estate of Stanley Spencer, all rights reserved, DACS 2000: cover, page 11.
Tate Publishing © Salvador Dali – Foundation Gala – Salvador Dali/DACS 2000: page 5(b).
Tate Publishing – Reproduced by permission of the Henry Moore Foundation: page 12(b).

Printed in the United States of America

1 2 3 4 5 6 7 8 9 05 04 03 02 01

20TH CENTURY ART

1920-40

REALISM *and* SURREALISM

Jackie Gaff

Gareth Stevens Publishing
A WORLD ALMANAC EDUCATION GROUP COMPANY

CONTENTS

A TIME FOR CHANGE.....................5

THE BAUHAUS 6

NEW OBJECTIVITY.......................8

STANLEY SPENCER 10

MOORE AND HEPWORTH...................12

THE REAL AMERICA.....................14

GEORGIA O'KEEFFE.....................16

MEXICAN MURALISTS 18

BEYOND REALITY.......................20

INTERNATIONAL SURREALISM 22

SALVADOR DALI 24

PICASSO'S GUERNICA...................26

THE ART OF REPRESSION................28

TIME LINE 30

GLOSSARY, BOOKS, AND WEB SITES 31

INDEX 32

Dictators came to power in several European countries by promising to solve the economic problems created by World War I. Benito Mussolini founded fascism in Italy, while Nazism flourished in Germany under Adolf Hitler. During the Spanish Civil War of 1936 to 1939, General Francisco Franco (below) became the leader of the government opposition. He remained dictator of Spain until his death in 1975.

A TIME FOR CHANGE

World War I devastated both the land and people of Europe. People around the globe desperately wanted change in order to learn from the past and build a new world from the rubble of the old.

Artists, too, found it a time to reassess. In the late 1800s and early 1900s, artists felt free to stop copying the colors and shapes of nature and became more expressive. Now, in the 1920s and 1930s, artists reconsidered their relationships with the great art of the past and explored their roles in modern society. Could art be relevant to everyday life? If so, how? Many artists felt it was time to revive the art style known as Realism, named because of its focus on the realities of life and living.

Other artists headed off completely in the opposite direction — into the world of dreams and the unconscious. Known as the Surrealists, these artists set out to make the real seem unreal, the natural seem unnatural, and the ordinary seem extraordinary!

Unemployment and inflation were widespread during the 1920s and 1930s, as nations struggled to deal with the mountain of debt that had built up during the war years.

One of the most extreme Surrealists, Salvador Dalí (1904–1989) created some of the wildest sculptures and paintings. Like many other Surrealists, Dali often combined everyday but unlikely objects — aiming to shock our senses and make us look at the world with fresh eyes.

LOBSTER TELEPHONE, *Salvador Dalí, 1936*

THE BAUHAUS

A German school of art, crafts, and architecture, called the Bauhaus, led the movement to make art more relevant in daily life. German-born architect Walter Gropius (1883–1969) founded the school in 1919.

SCHOOL OF THOUGHT

Gropius wanted to tighten the links between art, society, and industry. "The designer must breathe a soul into the dead product of the machine," he said. The Bauhaus pioneered the idea that an object's or a building's purpose should determine its form.

In 1925, Hungarian-born designer Marcel Breuer (1902–1981) followed the Bauhaus ideal of simplicity when he created the Model B3 chair, also known as the Wassily.

NOTHING BUT THE BEST

Gropius recruited some of the finest experimental artists of his day for the school, including American Lyonel Feininger (1871–1956), Russian-born Vasily Kandinsky (1866–1944), German-Swiss Paul Klee (1879–1940), and Hungarian-born László Moholy-Nagy (1895–1946). Along with the Bauhaus, the De Stijl movement in the Netherlands and the Constructivists in Russia believed in the purity and harmony of abstract art and its importance in building a brave, new, postwar Europe.

6

THE GOLDEN FISH
PAUL KLEE, 1925

Klee was one of the most popular instructors at the Bauhaus. He taugh the introductory design course as well as the stained-glass and weaving workshops. Although he was great friends with Kandinsky, Klee kept apart from most other teachers to avoid the school's internal politics. He was an individual in other ways as well. Unlike most Bauhaus artists his work was rarely totally abstract and always rooted in his love of nature. He described his art as "taking a line for a walk." His paintings are full of fantasy and childlike symbols and writing — which reflects the value he gave children's "power to see" and his fascination for the scientific study of nature and the universe.

Paul Klee, photographed in 192

MOVING STORY

The Brauhaus had a troubled history. Its avant-garde ideals conflicted with Germany's political ideals at the time. Although founded in Weimar, it was forced to move after the local government cut its funding. It moved to Dessau in 1925, but seven years later the Nazis closed the Dessau school. The Bauhaus opened for a while in Berlin, but the Nazis finally shut it down in 1933. During the 1930s, many of the Bauhaus teachers moved to the United States.

Designed by Walter Gropius, the simple geometric form of the Bauhaus building in Dessau reflected the school's key principle of "form following function."

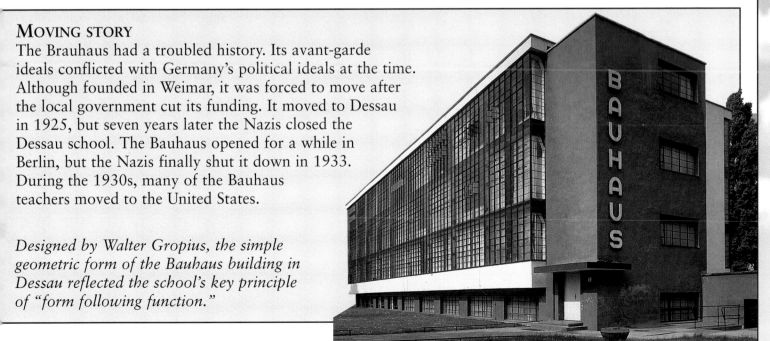

NEW OBJECTIVITY

Not all German artists shared the Bauhaus school's belief in the need for abstract art to contribute toward building a better world. Some artists criticized society instead of trying to rebuild it. Their particular version of Realism was expressed through representational art.

REALITY OF THE TIMES

Although their styles varied, German artists shared a detached and objective approach to their subjects. Because of this attitude, the movement became known as *Neue Sachlichkeit,* which is German for "new objectivity." Its most passionate artists were Otto Dix (1891–1969) and George Grosz (1893–1959). Both were brutally critical of the corruption in postwar Germany.

Brecht's The Threepenny Opera *opened in Berlin in August 1928.*

NIGHT AT THE OPERA

In musical plays such as *The Threepenny Opera*, German-born playwright and poet Bertolt Brecht (1898–1956) tried to show how money corrupts the rich and neglects the poor. Despite Brecht's attack on postwar Germany, the opera was an instant hit — especially with the wealthy classes it satirized.

Grosz's painting Pillars of Society *features two "captains of industry" (behind him). In 1932, driven out by the political situation in Germany, Grosz moved to the United States.*

SOCIETY PORTRAITS

The political and economic situation was extremely unstable in Germany throughout the 1920s and into the 1930s. While the poor suffered, others flaunted their wealth, power, or decadent lifestyles. Grosz's vision was of "mankind gone mad," and the chief targets for his caricatures were the wealthy people depicted in his painting *Pillars of Society* (1926) — army officers, priests, and the capitalists who had made fortunes supplying weapons and other equipment. He believed these people had either promoted or were profiting fom the horrors of war.

Dix, like Grosz, expressed his disgust with postwar Germany by showing the terrible nature of war and the decadence of bohemian life in Berlin, where the two artists lived. (The 1972 film *Cabaret* also portrayed the city in their day, but presented a kinder picture.) Dix focused his critical eye on the bitterness of the period. To Dix, Sylvia von Harden's tough, almost manly appearance symbolized a world gone crazy.

Although persecuted by the Nazis, Dix was one of the few avant-garde artists who didn't leave Germany in the 1930s.

PORTRAIT OF THE JOURNALIST SYLVIA VON HARDEN
OTTO DIX, 1926

STANLEY SPENCER

For some artists after World War I, an interest in Realism was based on their admiration for the great artists of the past. The avant-garde experiments of the 1900s and 1910s had shattered the traditions of Western painting and sculpture. Realism was a way for artists to reconnect 20th-century art to its roots.

Spencer carefully designed each painting by planning and drawing the composition first on paper. These drawings were then transferred to canvas, which he painted using diluted oil paints and fine, sable-hair brushes.

A LIVING TRADITION

British artist Stanley Spencer (1891–1959) was strongly inspired by the religious masterpieces of Giotto di Bondone (c. 1266–1337). Giotto was one of the first artists to break away from the thousand-year-old tradition in Western art of painting motionless, stylized figures and scenes. Instead, he tried to create the three-dimensional illusion of real life on a flat, two-dimensional surface, such as canvas.

A LIVING RELIGION

Like Giotto, Spencer wanted to show Christianity as a living, breathing, everyday experience. Spencer said his aim was to make "the inmost of one's wishes, the most varied religious feelings . . . an ordinary fact of the street." Spencer was born in the English village of Cookham where he spent most of his life. In his religious paintings, he retold the great stories of Christian history, setting them in Cookham and using the villagers as models.

MAN OF THE PEOPLE

Among Giotto's great achievements were the scenes from the lives of Christ and the Virgin Mary that he created on the walls of the Arena Chapel in Padua, in northeastern Italy. The painting to the left shows the dead Christ after he was taken down from the cross, surrounded by his mourning disciples. Unlike the emotionless figures that were common in artwork of Giotto's time, the people in his painting are full of life and feeling.

THE LAMENTATION OF CHRIST, *Giotto, c. 1306*

THE HOLINESS OF LIFE

The warm humanity and childlike qualities of Spencer's style made him one of the most distinctive and important British artists of the 20th century. Although most of his work retold religious stories, Spencer's sense of the holiness of life extended to the joy of simply being human. He expressed these feelings through paintings of nudes and of people going about their daily work, including a series of huge canvases showing shipbuilders during World War II on Scotland's River Clyde.

SAINT FRANCIS AND THE BIRDS
STANLEY SPENCER, 1935

Saint Francis of Assisi was born into a wealthy Italian family around 1181, but abandoned all his belongings during his twenties for total poverty in imitation of Christ. He went on to found a Roman Catholic order of nuns and friars called the Franciscans. Saint Francis was also famous for his love of birds, which is why Spencer painted him surrounded by ducks and geese in a 20th-century Cookham farmyard. Saint Francis is wearing slippers and a green bathrobe instead of his usual sandals and brown friar's habit. Saint Francis was based on Spencer's ageing and slightly forgetful father, William, who had begun wandering around Cookham dressed this way.

MOORE AND HEPWORTH

Two other British artists who admired the great art of the past were the abstract sculptors Henry Moore (1898–1986) and Barbara Hepworth (1903–1975).

Throughout his life, Moore mo[ved] freely between representation a[nd] abstraction. Abstraction could bring the viewer closer to realit[y], he said "away from a visual interpretation, but nearer to an emotional understanding."

RECUMBENT FIGURE
HENRY MOORE, 1938

Moore and Hepworth became famous for the holes they carved into their sculptures in the early 1930s. "A hole can have as much meaning as a solid mass," explained Moore. "There is a mystery in a hole in a cliff or hillside, in its depth and shape."

WORKING RELATIONSHIPS

Moore and Hepworth met after they began studying at the Leeds School of Art in 1919. They dated for a short time, but their relationship developed into a close friendship. The two artists' studies continued in London, where Moore, in particular, was inspired by the ancient stone sculptures that he saw at the British Museum. He admired how well each piece expressed emotions through the simplest of forms, as well as what he described as "its 'stoniness,' by which I mean its truth to material, its tremendous power."

NATURAL CONNECTIONS

The natural world — from wind- and water-eroded hills and cliffs to bones, pebbles, and shells — strongly influenced the work of Hepworth and Moore. They designed many of their sculptures to be enjoyed outdoors. Both carved their early sculptures directly into wood or stone, although in later years, they created works that were cast in metals, such as bronze.

Mayan chacmool, c. *10th–12th century*

CARVED IN STONE
At London's British Museum, Moore also studied sculptures known as *chacmools*. The Mayas, Toltecs, and other early Mexican peoples created these carvings of reclining male gods.

Hepworth created this tender stone sculpture in 1929, the year she gave birth to her son. Within a few years, Hepworth's work had become totally abstract and continued to be so for the rest of her life.

13

THE REAL AMERICA

In the United States, Realistic artists worked toward developing a uniquely American art, independent of European avant-garde movements. Artist Edward Hopper (1882–1967) summarized this when he stated his own goals: "Instead of subjectivity, a new objectivity. Instead of abstraction, a reaffirmation of representation. . . . Instead of internationalism, an art based on the American scene."

One of the major Realist of the 20th century, Hopper spent most of hi life in New York City. H visited Europe several times between 1906 and 1910 but remained unimpressed by the European avant-garde.

14

AMERICAN GOTHIC,
Grant Wood, 1930

Wood used his sister and his dentist as models for the couple in this tribute to the dignity of small-town life. The word Gothic *in the title refers to the architectural style of the house.*

AMERICAN TRADITION

Objective Realism was part of American art since the 1870s. However, in the early 20th century, a new group of artists created gritty depictions of everyday city life. They became known as the Ashcan School. (An ashcan is a garbage can.) Leaders of the Ashcan School included Robert Henri (1865–1929) and George Bellows (1882–1925), as well as Hopper.

TOWN AND COUNTRY

While artists such as Hopper focused on the poverty and loneliness of big towns and cities from the 1930s onward, other Realists celebrated the quiet, hard-working lifestyles of rural and small-town Americans. This back-to-the-earth movement was named Regionalism, and its chief exponents included Grant Wood (1892–1942) and Thomas Hart Benton (1889–1975).

DEPRESSING REALITY
The collapse of the New York Stock Exchange in the Wall Street Crash of 1929 began a time of hardship, first in the United States and then throughout the world. Regionalism was a way to provide faith in the American way of life in the face of national doubt, raised by widespread poverty.

NIGHTHAWKS, Edward Hopper, 1942

Although set in the United States, Hopper's haunting paintings go far beyond their period to reveal timeless truths about the loneliness and desolation of life in big cities and towns.

Many of Hopper's works have no people in them at all. When a work does have people, as in *Nighthawks*, the feeling of loneliness persists.

FREE SOUP &

Lines for food handouts were a common sight in the 1930s.

GEORGIA O'KEEFFE

Realism was not the only way for American artists during the 1920s and 1930s to express themselves. The work of Georgia O'Keeffe (1887–1986) moved between representation and abstraction. However, even in her most naturalistic paintings, making her subjects look lifelike was never her main concern.

HIDDEN TRUTHS

Instead, influenced by the ideas of the Russian-born pioneer of abstract art Vasily Kandinsky, O'Keeffe wanted to express the essential truths that lie beneath surface appearances. "Nothing is less real than realism . . ." stated O'Keeffe. "It is only by selection, by elimination, by emphasis that we get at the real meaning of things."

16

Founded in 1929, New York's Museum of Modern Art (MoMA) holds the world's largest and finest modern art collection. In 1946, O'Keeffe became the first woman artist to be honored with a major exhibition at MoMA.

MODERN LOVE STORY

O'Keeffe's career took off after some abstract drawings were shown to influential photographer and gallery owner Alfred Stieglitz (1864–1946). Stieglitz liked the drawings so much that he gave O'Keeffe her first one-woman show in 1917. In 1924, O'Keeffe and Stieglitz were married.

COW'S SKULL WITH CALICO ROSES
GEORGIA O'KEEFFE, 1932

Begun in the early 1930s, O'Keeffe's paintings of cow's skulls are among her most representational works. Some New Mexicans use artificial flowers in funerals, and for many people, the skull is a symbol of death. For O'Keeffe, though, the skull stood for life. She said she had used "the beautiful white bones" she had found in the desert "to say what is to me the wideness and wonder of the world as I live in it."

O'Keeffe was one of the most photographed women of her day.

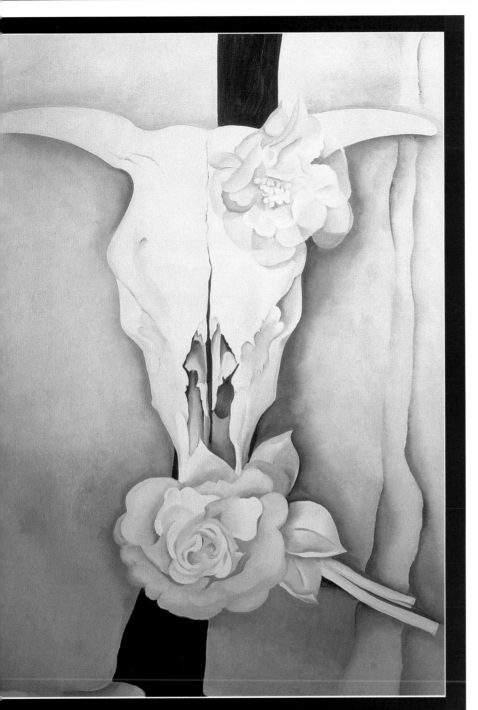

IN LOVE WITH THE LANDSCAPE

The pair lived in New York for most of the 1920s, but in 1929 O'Keeffe revisited a beloved landscape — the dramatic desert of southwestern New Mexico. From then on, O'Keeffe divided her time between New York, where her husband Stieglitz lived, and New Mexico, moving there permanently a few years after he died. The deep blue sky and the yellows, oranges, reds, and purples of the sand hills of the desert, together with the bleached bones and skulls she found there, remained O'Keeffe's main inspiration for the rest of her life.

PAYING PRECISE ATTENTION TO DETAIL

In the 1920s, O'Keeffe painted a number of New York scenes that are often described as Precisionist. This was an American art style which, influenced by photography and the fragmented style of Cubism, celebrated objects and industrial landscapes in a clear-cut, exact way. Besides O'Keeffe, leading Precisionists included Charles Demuth (1883–1935) and Charles Sheeler (1883–1965).

LANCASTER, *Charles Demuth*, 1920

MEXICAN MURALISTS

Another branch of Realism developed in Mexico during the 1920s. With their vast wall paintings, the Mexican muralists Diego Rivera (1886–1957), José Clemente Orozco (1883–1949), and David Alfaro Siqueiros (1896–1974) started the first major modern art movement to originate outside Europe.

LEANING TO THE LEFT

Since all three artists were committed to left-wing politics, their work was funded by Mexico's new socialist government, which was led by the art-loving President Álvaro Obregón. He came to power after a revolution overthrew the country's dictator, Porfirio Díaz.

18

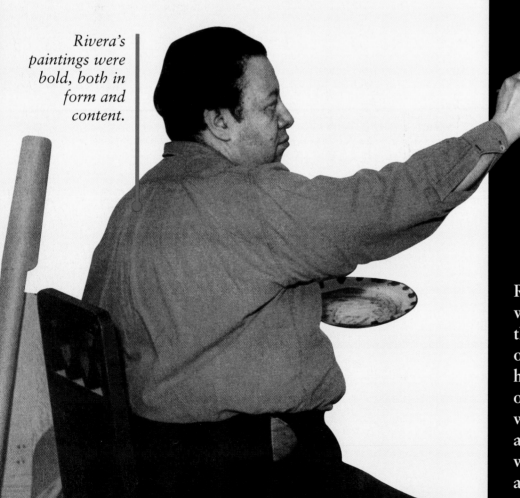

Rivera's paintings were bold, both in form and content.

SLAVERY IN THE SUGAR PLANTATION
DIEGO RIVERA, 1930–31

The striking painting on the right is part of a huge, 13-by-105-foot (4-by-32-meter) mural on the walls of the Palace of Cortés in Cuernavaca. Hernán Cortés, leader of the Spanish invaders who had conquered the Aztecs in the 1500s, had built the palace. For Rivera, the mural was an opportunity to turn a symbol of defeat into a memorial to victims of colonial oppression.

Rivera had experimented with Cubism in Paris during the 1910s. The major influence on his mural style, however, was his 1919 visit to Italy, where he was overwhelmed by the magnificent wall paintings created by Giotto and the great Italian masters who followed him in the 14th and 15th centuries.

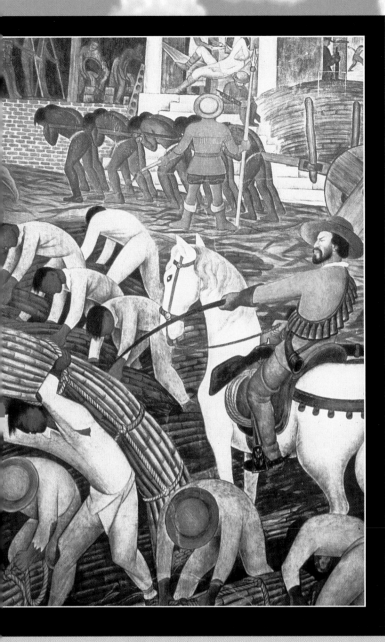

THE WRITING ON THE WALL

Obregón turned the walls of Mexico's schools, hospitals, and other public buildings over to Rivera, Orozco, and Siqueiros. He encouraged them to educate and inspire their fellow Mexicans by painting the story of their country's oppressed past and what everyone hoped would be a prosperous future. Although their individual styles varied, all three artists drew upon Mexican folk art and the art of their ancestors, the Mayans and the Aztecs.

19

ROCKY TIMES WITH THE ROCKEFELLERS

Rivera worked in the United States in the early 1930s and was hired in 1933 to create a mural for the Rockefeller Center in New York. This was surprising, since Rivera was a communist, and the Rockefellers were the world's richest oil family and leaders of Western capitalism. The project went well until the Rockefellers realized that the mural included a portrait of Lenin, the founder of Russian communism. They cancelled the project, paid off Rivera, and had his half-finished mural chiseled from the walls. This painting is of the mural's central character and is taken from Rivera's re-creation of the Rockefeller mural, done after he returned to Mexico in 1934.

MAN, CONTROLLER OF THE UNIVERSE, *Diego Rivera, 1934*

BEYOND REALITY

Back in Europe during the 1920s, writers and artists were exploring an alternative reality to the everyday world. By setting free the unconscious mind and the world of dreams, they hoped to create a kind of heightened, super reality. In French, *sur* means "above," and the movement was known as Surrealism.

Breton was regarded as the "Pope of Surrealism."

DEAD END OF DADA

The French poet and critic André Breton (1896–1966) started Surrealism in Paris in 1924. At first a literary movement, Surrealism grew out of Dada, which was an anti-art movement that was winding down by the early 1920s. Breton said that Dada had opened "wide the doors, but . . . they opened on to a corridor which was leading nowhere." Surrealists took what they believed to be the best of Dada — its shock tactics and love of nonsense — and focused on new forms of creativity.

CREATIVE ACCIDENTS

Breton was a great believer in tapping into his unconscious — "the absence of any control exercised by reason." A number of Surrealist artists, including Max Ernst (1891–1976), also tried to let ideas and images develop by chance, without conscious control. They called the process automatic drawing.

IN YOUR DREAMS

Another key influence was psychology, which is the science of the mind. The research of the meaning of dreams by Sigmund Freud (1856–1939), an Austrian psychoanalyst, fascinated the Surrealists. Dreams, Freud thought, could give us clues to our unconscious thoughts and desires.

Max Ernst had been one of the leaders of German Dadaism, attracted by Dada's revolt against conventional art. Ernst met Breton in 1921 and settled in Paris a year later, where his work focused on Surrealism.

FOREST AND DOVE
MAX ERNST, 1927

...st invented a number of forms of automatic painting. One form involved
...bing a pencil or charcoal on paper that has been laid over a rough surface.
...called this "frottage" (from *frotter*, French for "to rub"). Ernst named the
...nique he used for the background of *Forest and Dove* "grattage" (from *gratter*,
...ning "to scratch"). For this work, he laid a thickly painted but still wet canvas
...op of fish bones and pieces of wood and then scraped at the paint. After he
...n the painting, Ernst's imagination took over to create a lonely bird trapped
...le a cage — a prisoner in a nightmarish forest of looming, threatening trees.

INTERNATIONAL SURREALISM

In unlocking the unconscious, Surrealism was less of an art style than an attitude of mind, and the paintings and sculptures of individual artists varie enormously. Therefore, just as no two people dream the same dream, the paintings of Max Ernst, René Magritte (1898–1967), and Joan Miró (1893–1983 all look very different from one another.

TIME TRANSFIXED
RENÉ MAGRITTE, 1939

A toy-sized steam train puffs out of a fireplace — Magritte's style was detailed and realistic but his images were totally unreal. In other paintings, he turned clouds into loaves of French bread and rain into men in suits with bowler hats. In making the real unreal and the ordinary strange, his work was startling and often shocking or disturbing.

A man in a bowler hat first appeared in Magritte's paintings during the 1930s, sometimes as a self-portrait. Magritte also posed for photographs dressed in this outfit, as he did here.

NO PLACE LIKE HOME

Surrealism attracted artists of many nationalities. Some were based in Paris, but others lived and worked outside France. Magritte, for example, was born in Belgium and lived there most of his life, except for a brief time in Paris during the 1920s. Miró was a Spaniard who, until the mid-1930s, divided his year between Paris and his family's farm at Montroig, which is near Barcelona.

A WORLD OF TALENT

Other leading Surrealists included American Man Ray (1890–1976), Frenchmen Hans Arp (1887–1966) and André Masson (1896–1987), French-born Americans Yves Tanguy (1900–1955) and Marcel Duchamp (1887–1968), Chilean Roberto Matta (b. 1911), German-Swiss Meret Oppenheim (1913–1985), British-born Mexican Leonora Carrington (b. 1917) and Spaniard Salvador Dalí (1904–1989).

RANGE OF INTERESTS

For some artists, Surrealism was a short phase, but for many, it was their life's work. That life's work covered a wide range of art forms, from poetry and prose to painting, sculpture, photography, and filmmaking. Miró was a painter, sculptor, designer, and ceramist, while Magritte painted, sculpted, and made films.

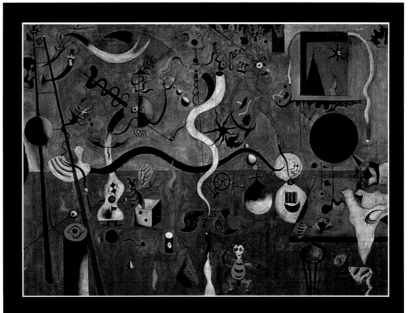

HARLEQUIN'S CARNIVAL
JOAN MIRÓ, 1924–1925

Miró was one of a few Surrealists whose work tended to be abstract. His paintings are full of bizarre shapes, many of which look like animals or microscopic organisms. For example, strange, insectlike creatures dance and make music in *Harlequin's Carnival,* while an ear is attached to the top of the ladder on the left. Miró said that his "hallucinations brought on by hunger" inspired the painting. This kind of abstraction is known as biomorphic, because the forms are based on the shape of living creatures instead of on geometric shapes.

Miró was mostly living on the island of Majorca by the time this photograph was taken in the 1970s.

SALVADOR DALÍ

The most famous — and most infamous — Surrealist of all was the Spaniard Salvador Dalí. Joining the movement in 1929, Dali was thrown out ten years later for two reasons: His work was becoming more focused on what sells than on pure art, and Breton objected to Dalí's right-wing political views and felt that Dalí's style was becoming too traditional.

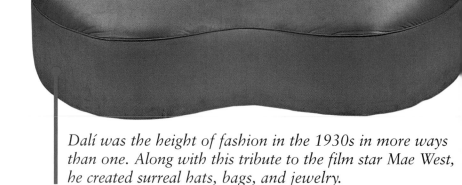

Dalí was the height of fashion in the 1930s in more ways than one. Along with this tribute to the film star Mae West, he created surreal hats, bags, and jewelry.

24

AN ARTIST FOR ALL MODES

Among the many outlets for Dalí's creative energy was set design for modern ballets. These included *Bacchanale*, which opened in New York in 1939, and *Ballet of Gala*, which premiered in Venice in 1961. Gala was the name of Dalí's wife.

A gigantic eye with a clock as its pupil dominated Dalí's set designs for Ballet of Gala.

ALL THE WORLD'S A STAGE

Dalí was a master at promoting himself and his work, often through outrageous stunts. In 1936, for example, he gave a lecture wearing a diving suit and nearly suffocated. As a result, he rapidly became extremely fashionable and wealthy, prompting Breton to nickname him "Avida Dollars," an anagram of Salvador Dalí.

A MINE OF CREATIVITY

Above all, Dalí was wildly inventive, with a passion for everything from painting and sculpture to fashion design, writing, and filmmaking. He cowrote the first Surrealist film, the gruesome *Un Chien Andalou* (1928) with the Spanish director Luis Buñuel (1900–1983). Dalí's work was sometimes hilariously funny, but more often, it was full of terror and violence. "The only difference between me and a madman is that I am not mad," he once said, and most of his paintings are nightmare visions of a drooping, melting, rotting world

APPARITION OF FACE AND FRUIT DISH ON A BEACH
SALVADOR DALÍ, 1938

Dalí described his paintings as "hand-painted dream photographs," and no matter how fantastic his imagery, his style was always realistic. He often played visual tricks as shown in this work, making pictures that portray more than one thing at once. Here, a ghostly face dissolves into a tall glass dish of fruit on a beach that folds down on the right like a tablecloth. The nose, mouth, and chin of the face are also the back of a seated woman, while the landscape toward the top is also a dog — its head faces to the right, and its collar is a bridge.

Dalí's wife Gala (c. 1884–1982) was his manager and his muse. She's the one in the fencing mask in this early 1940s photo of the famous pair.

PICASSO'S GUERNICA

Whether or not Dalí was mad may have been debatable — that the world was going mad during the 1930s seemed certain. While Hitler and Mussolini grew even more powerful in Germany and Italy, Spain was torn apart by the civil war between Franco's right-wing Nationalists and their opponents, the Republicans.

THE MADNESS OF WAR

Acting as Franco's allies, the Nazis bombed and virtually destroyed the northern Spanish town of Guernica on April 26, 1937. This atrocious act shocked the world and spurred the creation of one of its most devastating condemnations of violence — the painting *Guernica* by the great Spanish artist Pablo Picasso (1881–1973).

Bullfighting, the national sport of Spain, inspired two of the main images in Guernica — *the horse and the bull. Picasso was very passionate about bullfighting, attending fights whenever he could and celebrating them in a number of paintings.*

Republican troops prepare for an attack.

A NATION AT WAR, A PEOPLE DIVIDED
The Spanish Civil War was the height of a struggle between the supporters and opponents of the Republican government that was set up in 1931 to replace the rule of King Alfonso XIII. Fighting broke out in 1936 and ended three years later when the Nationalists captured the capital, Madrid. Thousands of soldiers and civilians died. General Franco ruled Spain as a dictator until he died in 1975.

GUERNICA
PABLO PICASSO, 1937

Painted entirely in black, gray, and white, *Guernica* is huge, about 12 by 16 feet (3.5 by 7.8 meters). It went far beyond portraying the specific event of the town's bombing and symbolized the madness, terror, and suffering of all war by its distorted animals and people. At its heart is the screaming horse, which the artist said represented the people, while the bull to its left stood for "brutality and darkness."

REPUBLICAN SYMPATHIES
Picasso was living in Paris when the Spanish Civil War began in 1936. Since he supported the Republicans, they asked him to plan a painting for the Spanish Pavilion at the Paris International Exhibition opening in July 1937. When news of the bombing of Guernica reached him, it inspired him to create a totally different painting.

THE LONG JOURNEY HOME
Picasso didn't want *Guernica* to be shown in Spain while Franco was in power. The painting was shipped to New York's Museum of Modern Art in the late 1930s. It wasn't until 1981 that the painting reached the Prado Museum in Madrid, Spain — eight years after Picasso's death and six years after Franco's.

The Nazis bombed Guernica for four hours, destroying 70 percent of the town's buildings and killing more than one thousand of its seven thousand citizens.

THE ART OF REPRESSION

Politics played a far more active role than simply inspiring great works like *Guernica* during the 1930s. Politicians in Germany and the Soviet Union tried to enforce the art styles that best served their political beliefs.

OUT WITH THE NEW, IN WITH THE OLD

Hitler came to power in Germany in 1933, while Joseph Stalin was virtual dictator of the Soviet Union from the late 1920s until his death in 1953. Both men knew how useful art could be. They also knew what they did and did not like — avant-garde was out, and classical or traditional Realism was in.

DEGENERATE ART

The Nazis labeled modern art *degenerate*, meaning "corrupt" or "degrading." To protest the art, they organized art shows to ridicule avant-garde artists and their work. The climax was the Munich Degenerate Art Exhibition of 1937, featuring works by over one hundred artists, including Ernst, Grosz, Klee, and Picasso.

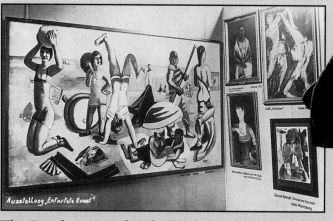

The Beach *(1921) by the leading German artist Max Beckmann (1884–1950) was included in the Degenerate Art Exhibition of 1937.*

WORKER AN
COLLECTIVE FAR
WOMAN, Ve
Mukhina, 19.

*This steel stat
of worke
towered abo
visitors to t
Soviet Pavili
at the 1937 Pa
Internation
Exhibitio*

28

R KIND OF ART OR NO ART!

s Realism wasn't to be used for the kind
ocial criticism practiced by George Grosz
Otto Dix. Instead, Realistic artists were
posed to produce idealized portraits of
scular workers and supposedly happy
man and Soviet families.

Artists who didn't create government-
approved work had their art destroyed or
banned from museums and art galleries. Some
artists were persecuted — the ones who upset
Stalin were sent to Siberian labor camps —
while others either went into hiding or chose
to emigrate, many to the United States.

KAHLENBERG FARMER'S FAMILY
ADOLF WISSEL, 1939

Hitler persecuted the Jews, believing that the
Aryan race of northern Europe was superior
to all other races and that German people
were the purest example of the Aryan race.

Nazi Germany encouraged artists to promote
this idea of racial superiority through images
of "pure-blooded" German families, like the
one shown in this painting, at work and play.

29

	ART	WORLD EVENTS	DESIGN	THEATRE & FILM	BOOKS & MUSIC
1920	•*Canadian Group of Seven formed*	•*U.S.: women over 21 get vote*	•*Edwin Lutyens: Cenotaph in London*	•*Eugene O'Neill:* Beyond the Horizon	•*Edith Wharton:* The Age of Innocence
1921	•*Max Ernst's Surrealist* Elephant of Celebes	•*Chinese communist party founded*	•*Germany: Mendelsohn's Einstein Tower*	•*Rudolph Valentino stars* The Sheik	
1922	•*Picasso's Neoclassical Women on the Beach*	•*Russia becomes USSR*	•*De Stijl founder van Doesburg at Bauhaus*	•*Murnau's chilling horror film* Nosferatu	•*James Joyce:* Ulysses •*T.S. Eliot:* The Waste Land
1923	•*Duchamp:* The Bride Stripped Bare	•*Italy: Mussolini seizes power*	•*Le Corbusier:* Towards a New Architecture	•*George Bernard Shaw:* Saint Joan	•*W.B. Yeats wins Nobel Prize for Literature*
1924	•*Paris: Breton's first Surrealist manifesto*	•*Britain: first Labour government elected*	•*Netherlands: Rietveld's Schröder House*	•*O'Casey:* Juno and the Paycock •*MGM formed*	•*E.M. Forster:* Passage to India
1925	•*Paris: first Surrealist exhibition*	•*Iran: Reza Khan rules as shah*	•*Paris: international exhibition of Art Deco*	•*Sergei Eisenstein:* The Battleship Potemkin	•*Franz Kafka:* The Trial •*Berg's opera* Wozzeck
1926	•*Grosz:* Pillars of Society •*Death of Claude Monet*	•*Britain: General Strike*	•*Bauhaus designer Marcel Breuer's Model B3 chair*	•*Fritz Lang's futuristic* Metropolis	•*Gide:* The Counterfeiters •*Milne:* Winnie-the-Pooh
1927	•*Ernst's frottage:* Forest and Dove	•*German stock market collapses*	•*U.S.: Fuller's Dymaxion House*	•*First successful "talkie":* The Jazz Singer	•*Kern and Hammerstein's hit musical* Show Boat
1928	•*Demuth:* I Saw the Figure 5 in Gold	•*USSR: Stalin's first five-year plan*	•*U.S.: van Alen's Art Deco Chrysler Building*	•*Buñuel and Dalí's* Un Chien Andalou	•*Bertolt Brecht's* The Threepenny Opera
1929	•*New York: founding of MoMA*	•*U.S.: Wall Street Crash; Hoover elected president*	•*Le Corbusier's Cubist Villa Savoye (to 1931)*	•*Best Picture Academy Award:* Broadway Melody	•*Virginia Woolf:* A Room of One's Own
1930	•*Grant Wood:* American Gothic	•*India: Gandhi leads Salt March protest*	•*Britain: Lutyen's Castle Drogo (from 1910)*	•*Dietrich:* The Blue Angel •*Coward:* Private Lives	•*Dashiell Hammett:* The Maltese Falcon
1931	•*Rivera: murals in Palace of Cortez*	•*Japanese army occupies Chinese Manchuria*	•*New York: Empire State Building completed*	•*Cagney:* The Public Enemy •*Lugosi's* Dracula	•*Deaths of Nellie Melba and Kahlil Gilbran*
1932	•*O'Keeffe:* Cow's Skull with Calico Roses	•*Nazis take control of Reichstag (parliament)*	•*Britain: Anglepoise lamp by Carwardine*	•*Johnny Weissmuller in* Tarzan, the Ape Man	•*Huxley:* Brave New World •*Porter:* "Night and Day"
1933	•*Germany: suppression of "degenerate art"*	•*Hitler in power as Chancellor of Germany*	•*Berlin: Bauhaus School closed by Nazis*	•*Wray:* King Kong •*Marx Brothers:* Duck Soup	•*Erskine Caldwell:* God's Little Acre
1934	•*U.S.:* The Machine *exhibition at MoMA*	•*China: Communists led by Mao on Long March*	•*Britain: Coates's Bakelite Ekco AD65 radio*	•*Shirley Temple, age 6, in* Stand Up and Cheer	•*Rachmaninov:* Rhapsody on a Theme of Paganini
1935	•*Spencer:* Saint Francis and the Birds	•*Italy invades Abyssinia (Ethiopia)*	•*U.S.: Raymond Loewy's Coldspot refrigerator*	•*Fred Astaire and Ginger Rogers star in* Top Hat	•*Benny Goodman called* "King of Swing"
1936	•*London: International Surrealist Exhibition*	•*Spanish Civil War begins* •*Edward VIII abdicates*	•*Volkswagen Beetle designed by Porsche*	•*Charlie Chaplin stars in* Modern Times	•*Spanish poet García Lorca executed in Civil War*
1937	•*Picasso responds to Nazi bombing with* Guernica	•*India: Congress Party wins elections*	•*U.S.: Frank Lloyd Wright's Falling Water*	•*Disney:* Snow White •*Renoir:* Grande Illusion	•*Agatha Christie:* Death on the Nile
1938	•*Moore:* Recumbent Figure	•*Germany and Austria unite (Anschluss)*	•*Finland: Alvar Aalto's Villa Mairea (to 1941)*	•*Hitchcock:* The Lady Vanishes •*Wilder:* Our Town	•*Jean-Paul Sartre:* Nausea •*du Maurier:* Rebecca
1939	•*Dalí expelled from Surrealist movement*	•*Spanish Civil War ends* •*Start of World War II*	•*Futuristic designs at New York World's Fair*	•*The Wizard of Oz and* Gone With the Wind	•*John Steinbeck:* The Grapes of Wrath

GLOSSARY

abstract art: art that does not attempt to represent the real world but that instead expresses meaning or emotion through shapes and colors.

Aryan: according to Nazism, a white, non-Jewish person. Aryans were supposedly intellectually and physically superior to all other races.

avant-garde: having, or pioneering the development of, new, bold, or experimental styles or techniques.

capitalism: an economic system in which individuals own the means of production, and the market determines economic decisions.

communism: a political and social system that promotes shared work and shared wealth, abolishing private property in favor of collective ownership.

Cubism: a modern art style that featured abstract geometric shapes and fragmented forms.

Dada: an antisense and antitradition movement in art and literature born in Europe and the United States during World War I.

fascism: a dictatorial political system that enforces state control of all aspects of society.

propaganda: the spreading of ideas, information, or rumors to help or injure a cause or institution. During war, governments use propaganda to convince people of the value of their side.

representational art: art that portrays things seen in the real world. Also known as figurative art.

socialism: an economic system in which the government owns the means of production and makes all economic decisions for a country.

unconscious: as proposed by Sigmund Freud, the part of the mind that people are usually unaware of but that often affects their thoughts and behavior.

MORE BOOKS TO READ

20s and 30s: Between the Wars. 20th Century Design. Jackie Gaff (Gareth Stevens)

Art Revolutions: Surrealism. Art Revolutions (series). Linda Bolton (Peter Bedrick Books)

Barbara Hepworth. The World of Art (series). Abraham Marie Hammacher (Thames and Hudson)

Diego Rivera. Junior World Biographies (series). David Shirley (Chelsea House)

Edward Hopper: The Art and the Artist. Gail Levin (W.W. Norton and Company)

The Essential René Magritte. The Essential (series). Todd Alden (Andrews McMeel Publishing)

Georgia O'Keeffe: An Adventurous Spirit. First Books (series). Philip Brooks (Franklin Watts)

Mexican Muralists: Orozco, Rivera, Siqueiros. Desmond Rochfort (Chronicle Books)

Miro. Famous Artists (series). Nicholas Ross, Antony Mason, Andrew S. Hughes, and Jen Green (Barrons Juveniles)

Salvador Dáli: Spanish Painter. Hispanics of Achievement (series). David Cater (Chelsea House)

WEB SITES

The Ashcan Artists. *nmaa-ryder.si.edu/collections/ exhibits/metlives/ashcanintrol.html*

Salvador Dáli. *www.mcs.csuhayward.edu/~malek/Dali.html*

Diego Rivera Web Museum. *www.diegorivera.com/index.html*

Surrealism. *library.thinkquest.org/J002045F/surrealism.htm*

Due to the dynamic nature of the Internet, some web sites stay current longer than others. To find additional web sites, use a reliable search engine with one or more of the following keywords: *abstract art, Ashcan School, Bauhaus, Mexican murals, Precisionism, Realism, Regionalism, sculpture, Surrealism,* and the names of individual artists.

INDEX

abstract art 5, 6, 8, 12, 13, 14, 16, 23
Alfaro Siqueiros, David 18, 19
American art 14, 16
American Gothic 14
Apparition of Face and Fruit Dish on a Beach 25
Arp, Hans 23
Ashcan School 14
automatic painting 20, 21
automatism 20

Bacchanale 24
Ballet of Gala 24
Bauhaus 6-7, 8
Beach, The 28
Beckmann, Max 28
Bellows, George 14
Benton, Thomas Hart 14
biomorphic abstraction 23
Brecht, Bertolt 8
Breton, André 20, 24
Breuer, Marcel 6
British Museum 13
Buñuel, Luis 24

Cabaret 9
capitalism 19
Carrington, Leonora 23
chacmools 13
Chien Andalou, Un 24
Clemente Orozco, José 18, 19
communism 19
Constructivism 6
Cortés, Hernán 18
Cow's Skull with Calico Roses 16-17
Cubism 17, 18

Dada 20
Dalí, Gala 24, 25

Dalí, Salvador 5, 23, 24-25, 26
De Stijl 6
Degenerate Art Exhibition 28
Demuth, Charles 17
Díaz, Porfirio 18
Dix, Otto 8, 9, 29
Duchamp, Marcel 23

Ernst, Max 20, 21, 22, 28

fascism 4
Feininger, Lyonel 6
Forest and Dove 21
France 23
Franco, General Francisco 4, 26, 27
Freud, Sigmund 20
frottage 21

geometric forms 7, 23
Germany 4, 7, 8, 9, 26, 28, 29
Giotto di Bondone 10, 11, 18
Golden Fish, The 6-7
grattage 21
Gropius, Walter 6, 7
Grosz, George 8, 9, 28, 29
Guernica 26-27, 28

Harlequin's Carnival 23
Henri, Robert 14
Hepworth, Barbara 12-13
Hitler, Adolf 4, 26, 28, 29
Hopper, Edward 14, 15

Italy 4, 11, 18, 26

Kahlenberg Farmer's Family 29
Kahlo, Frida 19

Kandinsky, Vasily 6, 16
Klee, Paul 6, 7, 28

Lamentation of Christ, The 10-11
Lancaster 17
Lobster Telephone 5
London 13

Mae West Lips Sofa 24
Magritte, René 22, 23
Man, Controller of the Universe 19
Masson, André 23
Matta, Roberto 23
Mexico 18, 19
Miró, Joan 22, 23
Model B3 chair 6
Moholy-Nagy, László 6
Moore, Henry 12-13
Mother and Child 13
Mukhina, Vera 28
murals 18, 19
Museum of Modern Art (MoMA) 16, 27
Mussolini, Benito 4, 26

Nazis 4, 7, 9, 26, 27, 29
Neue Sachlichkeit (New Objectivity) 8
New York 14, 15, 16, 17, 19, 24, 27
Nighthawks 15

Obregón, Álvaro 18,19
O'Keeffe, Georgia 16-17
Oppenheim, Meret 23

Paris 18, 20, 23, 27, 28
Paris International Exhibition 27, 28
Picasso, Pablo 26, 27, 28
Pillars of Society 8
Portrait of the Journalist Sylvia von Harden 9

Prado Museum 27
Precisionists 17

Ray, Man 23
Realism 5, 8, 10, 14, 16, 18, 28, 29
Recumbent Figure 12
Regionalism 14
religious art 10
representational art 8, 12, 14, 16
Rivera, Diego 18, 19
Rockefeller Center 19

Saint Francis and the Birds 11
sculptures 5, 10, 12, 13, 22, 23
Sheeler, Charles 17
Slavery in the Sugar Plantation 18-19
Spain 4, 26
Spanish Civil War 4, 26, 27
Spencer, Stanley 10-11
Stalin, Joseph 28, 29
Stieglitz, Alfred 16, 17
Surrealism 5, 20, 22, 23, 24

Tanguy, Yves 23
Threepenny Opera, The 8
Time Transfixed 22

United States 7, 8, 14, 15, 18, 19, 29
USSR 28

Wall Street Crash of 1929 14
West, Mae 24
Wissel, Adolf 29
Wood, Grant 14
Worker and Collective Farm Woman 28
World War I 4, 5, 10